Discovery™

I Am a
SHARK

Level 2

Written by Lori C. Froeb

Silver Dolphin

P1 PRE-LEVEL 1: ASPIRING READERS

1 LEVEL 1: EARLY READERS

2 LEVEL 2: DEVELOPING READERS

- Simple factual texts with mostly familiar themes and content
- Concepts in text are supported by images
- Includes glossary to reinforce reading comprehension
- Repetition of basic sentence structure with variation of placement of subjects, verbs, and adjectives
- Introduction to new phonic structures
- Integration of contractions, possessives, compound sentences, and some three-syllable words
- Mostly easy vocabulary familiar to kindergarteners and first-graders

3 LEVEL 3: ENGAGED READERS

4 LEVEL 4: FLUENT READERS

Silver Dolphin Books
An imprint of Printers Row Publishing Group
A division of Readerlink Distribution Services, LLC
10350 Barnes Canyon Road, Suite 100, San Diego, CA 92121
www.silverdolphinbooks.com

ISBN: 978-1-68412-799-3
Manufactured, printed, and assembled in Shenzhen, China.
First printing, March 2019. RRD/03/19
23 22 21 20 19 1 2 3 4 5

I am a shark. There are over four hundred species of sharks on earth.

I am a great white shark. I am the largest **predator** in the ocean!

Sharks have been around for a long time.

We have been around for more than four hundred million years!

My biggest **ancestor** was megalodon.

Scientists believe megalodon grew up to sixty feet long.

That's longer than a school bus!

Here is a megalodon tooth next to one of my teeth.

Many scientists believe megalodon was the largest fish to ever live.

Great white sharks are probably the most famous sharks.

We have even been in many movies!

But sharks come in many shapes and sizes.

This is a whale shark. She is the biggest fish in the world!

She may be big, but she eats tiny creatures called **plankton**.

plankton

This is a hammerhead.

His head shape lets him see **prey** better than other sharks.

He also uses his head to catch food. He pins down prey in the sand then eats it.

This is a zebra shark.

She has spots now, but when she was born she had stripes like a zebra.

The zebra shark spends most of her time on the ocean floor.

This is a thresher shark.
Check out that long tail.

The thresher uses his
tail to stun fish by
slapping them.

Sharks come in different shapes and sizes, but we have many things in common.

All sharks are fish. All sharks are cold-blooded.

Our bodies are the same temperature as the water around us.

Sharks don't have bones. Instead, our skeletons are made out of **cartilage**.

Cartilage is flexible and light.

It makes it easier to swim faster and longer.

Every shark has these basic parts:

nose
Sharks have an amazing sense of smell.

eyes
Sharks have eyes, but no eyelids.

gill slits
Sharks can have five, six, or seven gill slits on each side.

jaws
The jaws can move forward to grab prey. Most animal jaws only move up and down.

pectoral fins
These fins help the shark move up and down.

caudal fin
This tail fin moves back and forth to make the shark move forward.

dorsal fin
These fins keep the shark from rolling over.

pelvic fins
These fins help the shark steer and stop.

We have scales like other fish.

Our scales are called **dermal denticles**. Denticle means "little tooth."

The denticles make shark skin feel like sandpaper.

They make water move over our bodies faster.

To pick up speed, we use our tail fins.

Every species of shark has a different-shaped tail fin.

We move our tail fins back and forth to go forward.

great white shark

blacktip reef shark

hammerhead shark

thresher shark

15

All sharks have sharp teeth—lots of them!

This is a good thing because our teeth fall out often.

tiger shark

great white shark

bull shark

mako shark

oceanic whitetip shark

When one tooth falls out, another moves into its place.

A great white can have three hundred teeth in its jaws at one time.

During my lifetime, I may go through thirty thousand teeth.

Adult humans only have thirty-two teeth. If one falls out, it is not replaced.

Most sharks are born alive, but some hatch from egg cases.

A catshark laid these egg cases.

Baby sharks are called pups.

You can see the pups growing inside.

adult catshark

Shark pups that are born alive have an extra challenge.

They must swim away quickly or their mother may eat them.

I was one of those pups!

Great whites like me like to hang out in the shallow parts of the oceans all around the world.

We like the warmer water that is found there.

But we also travel to deeper water and further out to sea.

Usually, I follow my nose to where the food is!

Sharks have an amazing sense of smell.

We can sniff tiny amounts of blood in the water to find prey.

My nose will even tell me which direction the scent is coming from.

Take a close look at my nose.

See those small dots?

They are organs that can feel electrical fields in the water.

Sharks can detect a fish's heartbeat if it is nearby.

Like all sharks, I am a **carnivore**. This means I eat meat.

Here are some of my favorite foods:

dolphins

sea lions

sea turtles

tuna

rays

Sometimes other sharks!

We do not hunt humans for food.

Sometimes we attack a human by mistake.

Our only predators are humans.

They kill more than one hundred million of us a year.

When I hunt, I usually stay above or below my prey.

My belly is white and my back is dark gray.

I am hard to see in the deep water from above.

I am also hard to see in the sunlit water from below.

This is called **countershading**.

I can surprise my prey
because it doesn't see me.

I can surprise my prey another way.

I **breach** to hunt seals near the surface.

To breach, I swim up fast from below the seal.

I am so fast that I fly into the air after grabbing the seal.

I splash back into the water and enjoy my meal.

Great whites are one of the only shark species that do this.

All this talk about hunting has made me hungry!

I am going to go grab something to eat.

See you later!

Super Shark Stats!

Fastest

The mako shark can swim sixty miles per hour. That is as fast as a car on the highway!

Toothiest

A bull shark can have three hundred fifty teeth in its mouth at one time.

Biggest

The whale shark can weigh as much as four elephants.

Hardest to Spot

The wobbegong shark uses **camouflage** to blend in with the seafloor. Can you find it?

Glossary

ancestor: a creature that lived in the past, a relative

breach: to swim upward fast enough to leave the water

camouflage: an animal's coloring that helps it hide and blend in

carnivore: an animal that eats meat

cartilage: a light, rubbery material from which a shark's skeleton is made

countershading: a type of camouflage where the bottom of the body is light and the top is dark

dermal denticles: tiny toothlike scales covering a shark's skin

plankton: tiny animals that float near the ocean's surface

predator: an animal that hunts other animals for food

prey: an animal that is hunted by other animals for food